W9-BHJ-565

Bannockburn School Dist. 106
2165 Telegraph Road
Bannockburn, Illinois 60015

DUE

Using Water

Andrew Einspruch

Bannockburn School Dist. 106
2165 Telegraph Road
Bannockburn, Illinois 60015

This edition first published in 2011 in the United States of America by Smart Apple Media. All rights reserved. No part of this book may be reproduced in any form or by any means without written permission from the publisher.

Smart Apple Media
P.O. Box 3263
Mankato, MN, 56002

First published in 2010 by
MACMILLAN EDUCATION AUSTRALIA PTY LTD
15–19 Claremont St, South Yarra, Australia 3141

Visit our web site at www.macmillan.com.au or go directly to www.macmillanlibrary.com.au

Associated companies and representatives throughout the world.

Copyright © Andrew Einspruch 2010

Library of Congress Cataloging-in-Publication Data

Einspruch, Andrew.
    Using water / Andrew Einspruch.
        p. cm. — (Living sustainably)
    Includes index.
    ISBN 978-1-59920-558-8 (library binding)
    1. Water conservation—Juvenile literature. 2. Water-supply—Juvenile literature. 3. Water use—Juvenile literature.
    I. Title. TD495.E43 2011
    333.91'16—dc22
                        2009045104

Publisher: Carmel Heron   Designer: Kerri Wilson (cover and text)
Managing Editor: Vanessa Lanaway   Page layout: Kerri Wilson
Editor: Laura Jeanne Gobal   Photo Researcher: Jes Senbergs (management: Debbie Gallagher)
Proofreader: Helena Newton   Illustrator: Robert Shields
                                          Production Controller: Vanessa Johnson

Manufactured in China by Macmillan Production (Asia) Ltd.
Kwun Tong, Kowloon, Hong Kong
Supplier Code: CP January 2010

Acknowledgments
The author and the publisher are grateful to the following for permission to reproduce copyright material:

Front cover photograph of saving water, courtesy of Newspix/Newsphotos/Chris Mangan.

Photographs courtesy of © Craig Lamotte/Corbis, 9; © Will & Deni McIntyre/Corbis, 13 (top); Rob Cruse, 15, 18 (all); Absodels/Getty Images, 26; L. Ancheles/Getty Images, 17; Digital Vision/Getty Images, 22; Sean Justice/Getty Images, 30; Christine Schneider/Getty Images, 14; Peter Ziminski/Getty Images, 4; © Ben Klaus/iStockphoto, 13 (bottom); Jupiter Images, 5, 6, 12, 13 (left); NASA, 8; © Newspix /News Ltd/Quest, 20; Newspix/News Ltd, 29; Newspix/News Ltd/Alex Coppel, 19; Newspix/News Ltd/Heidi Linehan, 21; Newspix/News Ltd/Richard Serong, 28; Photolibrary © Michael Austen/Alamy, 25; Photolibrary/Image Source, 27; Photolibrary/Jillian Winslow, 23; savewater!® Alliance Inc., www.savewater.com.au, 16.

While every care has been taken to trace and acknowledge copyright, the publisher tenders their apologies for any accidental infringement where copyright has proved untraceable. Where the attempt has been unsuccessful, the publisher welcomes information that would redress the situation.

Contents

When a word is printed in **bold**, you can look up its meaning in the Glossary on page 31.

Living Sustainably

Living sustainably means using things carefully so there is enough left for people in the future. To live sustainably, we need to look after Earth and its **resources**.

If we cut down too many trees now, there will not be enough lumber in the future.

The things we do make a difference. We can use water, energy, and other resources wisely. Our choices can help make a sustainable world.

The choices we make when we use water affect Earth in many ways.

Using Water

Water is a very useful resource. We use water for many activities, such as bathing, washing our clothes, and growing food. Water is a part of our daily lives.

Swimming is a fun way to use water.

Water is needed by all living things. We must have water to drink. Without water, all plants and animals will die.

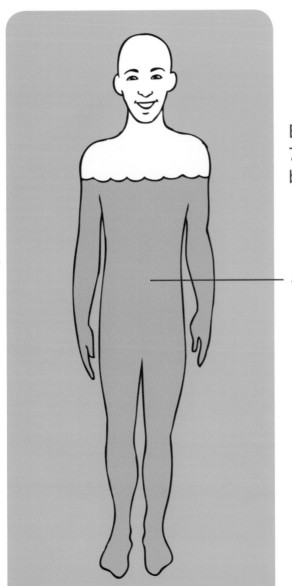

Between 55 and 70 percent of the human body is made of water.

55–70 percent water

Earth's Water

There is much more water than land on Earth. Oceans and seas cover more than two-thirds of Earth's surface.

This satellite image shows how much of Earth is covered by water.

Salty Water

Water from oceans and seas is salty. It cannot be used for drinking, bathing, or growing food. The only water we can use is **freshwater**.

Salty water from the sea and ocean can only be used once the salt has been removed.

The Water Cycle

The water cycle explains how water is always moving from one place to another in different forms. There are six main stages in the water cycle.

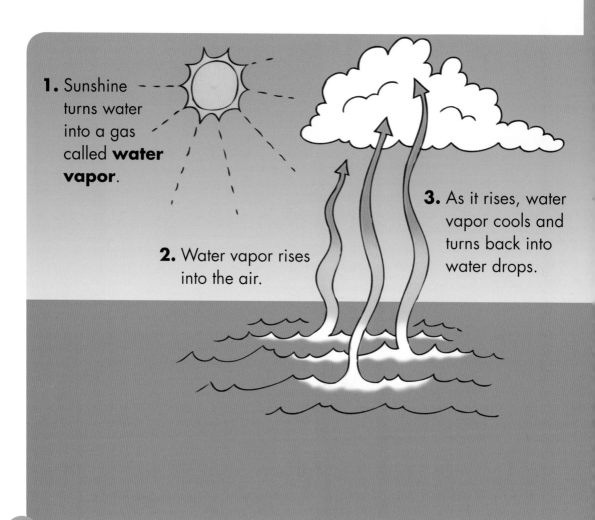

1. Sunshine turns water into a gas called **water vapor**.

2. Water vapor rises into the air.

3. As it rises, water vapor cools and turns back into water drops.

4. The water drops join together to form clouds.

5. When clouds get too heavy, rain falls.

6. Rainwater flows into rivers, which flow back to the ocean, and the cycle begins again.

Where Does Faucet Water Come From?

Faucet water begins its long journey to homes and other buildings at reservoirs. A reservoir is a man-made lake that holds freshwater until it is needed.

Water in reservoirs is piped to a big plant to be cleaned.

Clean water is pumped into storage tanks.

From storage tanks, water is piped to homes and other buildings.

Turn on the faucet and out comes water!

Using Water Sustainably

If everyone uses water sustainably, there will always be enough of it. The most important way to use water sustainably is to save it.

When we pour a cup of water, we should save what we do not drink for later.

Saving water means using less water. Saving water also means reusing water whenever we can.

Reuse bathwater by collecting it in buckets and watering the garden with it.

Save Water in the Kitchen

We can save water in the kitchen by putting an aerator on the kitchen faucet. Aerators reduce the flow of water out of the faucet.

When this aerator is fitted to a faucet, it will help save water.

We can also save water in the kitchen by:
- turning off faucets firmly so they do not drip
- washing dishes in a dishwasher or dishpan instead of under a running faucet

Save the cool water, which flows from the hot faucet first before the hot water arrives, for drinking.

Save Water in the Bathroom

In the bathroom, we can save water by changing the way we wash our hands.

1. Turn the faucet on and wet your hands.

2. Turn the faucet off and wash your hands with soap.

3. Turn the faucet on and rinse your hands.

We can also save water in the bathroom by:
- turning the faucet off while brushing our teeth
- taking short showers instead of baths
- collecting used bath and shower water in a bucket for the garden

Use a shower timer to help keep showers short.

Save Water in the Garden

To save water in the garden, plants should be watered early in the morning or in the evening. This stops water from being lost to **evaporation** under the hot sun.

Watering the garden at the right time of day can save a lot of water.

We can also save water in the garden by:
- collecting rainwater to use on the garden
- using **mulch** around plants to help trap water
- washing bicycles and pets on the lawn so the water soaks into the soil

Mulch shades the soil from the sun and helps reduce evaporation.

Save Water at School

We can save water at school by practicing the same water-saving rules we follow at home. Use less water and use it wisely.

Turn the faucet off firmly when you have finished washing your hands.

We can save water at school by:

- washing paintbrushes in a stoppered sink instead of under a running faucet
- bringing a water bottle to school instead of using a drinking fountain

Paintbrushes can also be soaked in a glass or bucket of water to remove paint.

Save Water in the Schoolyard

A lot of water can be wasted in the schoolyard. It is important to pay attention and spot any signs of waste, such as leaking faucets.

Size of leak	Water wasted	
	Per day	Per year
One drop of water per second	around ½ bucket	83 buckets
Drop breaking into a stream of water	10 buckets	3,650 buckets
0.06-inch stream (1.5-mm)	36 buckets	13,140 buckets
0.12-inch stream (3-mm)	110 buckets	40,150 buckets
0.24-inch stream (6-mm)	389 buckets	141,985 buckets

Note: 1 bucket = 2.1 gallons (8 liters)

The school garden can be watered with leftover water from water bottles. We can also catch rainwater in buckets or tanks and use it on the garden.

Watering the garden on cloudy days saves water as less water is lost through evaporation.

Using Bottled Water

Bottled water is drinking water that is sold in plastic or glass bottles. Water that is sold in plastic bottles creates a lot of waste.

Instead of buying bottled water, carry water in a reusable bottle when you leave home.

Some bottled water is shipped from places far away. Shipping uses Earth's oil resources and creates **pollution**.

The farther bottled water travels to reach us, the more resources it uses.

Share the Message

Being **water-smart** is an important message to share with your friends. Ask your teacher if your class can make posters about saving water to put up around the school.

Share the message about being water-smart with fun posters.

A Water-smart School

Newmarket State School in Queensland, Australia, is a water-smart school. A **donation** helped the school install water tanks and water-saving toilets.

Students from Newmarket State School are learning about their school's water-saving steps.

A Sustainable World

Saving water is one way to live sustainably.
How many ways can you save water today?
Our choices and actions will help make a
sustainable world.

Make a list of the things you can
do to use water sustainably.

Glossary

donation   money or items given to help a person or organization

evaporation   when water changes from a liquid to a vapor because of heat

freshwater   water that is not salty, usually from lakes and rivers

mulch   loose materials, such as woodchips or straw, spread over the ground to hold in moisture

pollution   waste that damages the air, water, or land

resources   useful things found on Earth that are hard to replace once they run out

water-smart   acting in a way that saves water

water vapor   water in the form of a gas

Index